© Roberta Lowing, 2021

This book is copyright. Apart from any fair dealing for the purposes of study and research, criticism, review, or as otherwise permitted under the Copyright Act, no part may be reproduced by any process without written permission. Inquiries should be made to the publisher.

National Library of Australia
Catalogue-in-Publication entry
Roberta Lowing
This Attic of Fire
ISBN: 978-0-6451365-4-8

Published by Apothecary Archive: 2021
Created on Gadigal land.
Book Design: Gareth Sion Jenkins
Typeset in Roboto: 10pt, 12pt, 14pt

This Attic of Fire

Roberta Lowing

CONTENTS

Epilogue: Against The Glass (Transantarctic Mountains, 2039)

I: The Hours And The Times 9

Photograph: *Sunrise, Syria, August 2017* 11
Quota 12
Deep Water 14
Slick 19
Dawn: Cordova Bay, Alaska 20
Embedded 22
Voyagers 26

II: A Walk In The World 28

Vacant Lot 29
Imaginal 30
Nightbirds 32
In The Laneway 34
Pole Star 36
The Pond-Moonlight 38
Touch 40
Let The Broken 42
Dragons 43
Do Not Read This Wall 44

III: The Animal Kind 45

Ego And The Possum 46
Hawk 48
Rattlesnake 50
Coyote 54
Pachyderm 56

IV: Black Sun 57

Climate Change 58
Hunting 59
What We Say When You Ask Why We Did What We Did 60
Windmill 62
Somersaults 63

V: Poems Written In The Time of Plague 65

Blue In The Time Of Plague 66
The Burn 68
Day 5: Second Contact 69
Holes 70
Half The Sky 72
Listening 73
Holy Mother In The Suburbs 74
Pebble 75
Sitting Alone 76
Music In The Time Of Plague 78

VI: It Starts Here 80

Democracy 81
Natalya Says Thank You 82
Three 84
The Last Poem 87

Acknowledgements/Notes 89

EPILOGUE: AGAINST THE GLASS (TRANSANTARCTIC MOUNTAINS, 2039)

We run into the ice tunnel.
The light is pewter, the air flint;
our breath bruises the walls.

The sulphur fires hunting us
reveal a thousand-roomed museum:
a canoe with fossil ferns in the bark,

the stilled hands of the bearded man
in the blue dark; his dog, ears forever
pricked, in a vault down the hall.

We run and as we run
we wonder, What did we know, *what
did we know*, obsessed as we were

with lighting our northern caverns?
We thought we could always escape
with sleight of hand: the doubled joint,

the key in the mouth.
But we were a carnival
applauding itself.

As the air grows a fiery crown,
we run through the last ice tunnel
to the underworld, where even Houdini
beats his hands against the glass.

~ I ~

The Hours And The Times

The past is only now reaching us.
Our last perfect place of exile
revealed for what it always was:
a gateway to the dead.

PHOTOGRAPH: *SUNRISE, SYRIA, AUGUST 2017*

At first, only desert: red-baked outer night,
mute churn of rock and cliff, weathered
by regimes of wind that tug and turn
the dead hawks hanging from telegraph poles,

black pennants celebrating the long burn
of nothing gained, or learnt.

Dawn severs the dark wire hieroglyphs
which fall, silenced, from the telegraph poles
onto highways of sand.
Wind rakes the cliffs through the frame,

throwing blades of dust
that cut your fingers to the quick.

Look deeper: there, the vast bird-less silence,
the inner night, the desert,
the clusters of knifepoints masquerading
as stars. There, the shadow in the rough tent:

a child, her skin corrugated by spine, a disjointed
line of bone curled on a hospital cot.

Even though her head is turned almost out of focus, follow
the curve of her eye: how wide, how
straining. The blink of an eyelash, slowing.
Her cold black hair is in pigtails,

rainbow elastic around each end,
pink plastic bobbles shiny
and clean. Maybe she polished them, maybe
she used to put the bobbles in her mouth. The comfort.

QUOTA

A scintilla, nothing in itself:
an ember flickering on hot draughts
inside the factory.

The golden flame sped over the oily concrete,
glittered above the greasy assembly trays, blew out
a ball of purple petrol fumes across the floor.

The fire doors had rusted shut long ago;
the main doors locked
until the workers reached the chassis quota.

["... Some were found
at their machines,
arms around the twisted steel.

Some—having climbed up to hack
through the small windows—
were melded with the rafters,
pinned angels in the smoke.

Some seared to death,
some were scalded.
Some burned from within
when their hearts caught fire.

Each was reduced
to the shadow of a child falling
across cracked pavement."]

Giant suns blaze on in the black sky.
The factory's twisted ribcage pincers the paddock
where every furrow has a body punctured

with flying bolts, broken glass, belt buckles ...
The man in the suit makes another list—*hydrocarbon
epoxy resin melted rubber*—on paper whiter than skin.

The crowd stands, silent,
swaying slightly. Every eye is dry
because of the heat. Even after twelve hours,

all the fire-fighters can do is wait
and watch their arcs of water
turn to scorched mist.

At the gate, the hot-dog seller sets up his van.
A baby sleeps, open-mouthed, on a blanket.
Radio static stutters between the endless, winking
line of car lights accelerating up the valley.

DEEP WATER

        I

    Morning
and the oil rig towers
over the water
a giant metal carapace
a locust where no insect should be
interested only in its shadow and its feeding tube
dropped five thousand feet into the sea

Men are tying up
and departing
drill ships sway on the horizon
seagulls and pelicans bend into a slow wind
a turtle turns over in the midstream current
the only sounds
the spangled rush of water
      a faint echo of voices carried
      forty miles offshore
threaded with marsh mud and egg shards

    Evening
and the oil rig sucks, pulls and feeds
the men constantly tying up, departing
oblivious to radiance below
where white-bellied starfish define
the outer reaches of sky
unblinking cuttlefish,
shark and dolphin, whale
nose the unharvested forests
swaying gently
      as blue shallows give way to electric green

II

What is the sound of the end?
Is it the faint moan far below
as the smile widens in the steel pipe?

III

The insect is wounded already
the pressure growing from the earth's skin
up through bloodied sea
a black breath able to rip away
jointed metal legs

Kneeling in the water over the untethered men
the insect is not dead
even when its heart fails two days later
the black blood will gush
        up through the length of its body

IV

On the sea floor five thousand feet below
the day begins   an imbalance of pressure
a blockage   a small explosion
        the day begins
all the devices fail
        the blow-out preventer
        the hydraulic systems   the intricate stack-slicing
shut-off mechanism

Far below the drilling platform
the riser pipe

damaged beyond knowing
opens itself three times to the dark sea

V

The sound of the apocalypse
is the silence of depleted souls
blackness leaking from slit veins
fish rolling in sulphurous rivers
blind assemblies rising
blackness rolling
stars going out one by one
the earth saying
enough

VI

The survivors depart
the mechanics   the miners   the welders
the cooks   the drill ship drivers
    Out of London and Washington
Baton Rouge and Key West
new men are tying on
    engineers
    deep sea divers   computer experts
accountants

Robots are deployed
mud is pumped into the blow-out preventer
    huge containment caps are designed
        to drop over the leaks and suck oil

The day continues

the robots fail in the cold water
the pressure is too great for the pump
the top-kill kills nothing but time
the submarine crashes into the containment cap
the squandered stars
fall away unnoticed

VII

The sea is on fire
flames rise from rainbow currents
infernos sway along the rim of the earth
restless   searching
the waves are tipped with yellow foam
tan-coloured booms coil around the coast
like mile-long water-snakes

VIII

The numbers are always tying up
and departing
April 20:
one thousand barrels leaking a day
(company estimate)
May 5:
five thousand barrels leaking a day
(revised company estimate)
May 8:
twelve thousand barrels a day
(observers' estimate)
May 29:
twenty-five thousand barrels a day
(scientists' estimate)
June 24:
fifty thousand barrels a day

IX

on the brown coast
between the tarred reeds
the starfish lies with its belly
turned to the sun
the turtle's eyes are pools of black
      the pelican drags
its weighted wings
across the inky land
leaving the figures with buckets and scrapers
to kneel on the sand.

SLICK

Standing on the shore,
you smell it long before you see it.
It exhales its name
on a hot unfamiliar wind,
the word oozing out of
the steel birth canal:
a black seed which tethers
orange-veined tendrils
to the ocean surface.
Soon it will abandon the rig's pylons
to answer the siren call of the shore
a hundred kilometres away:
lapping turquoise shallows,
pearl beaches, sun-warmed wings
of drowsing birds.
Dragging a shroud made phlegmy
by the mix of blood and body,
it gives birth and digs graves
in the same moment,
the odour wrecking in
your sodden mouth long before
you discover the roughly bandaged wounds,
the yellow cuts that fester under cheap remedies.
So comes the word, black and gelatinous,
waving its limbs of orange mist,
not needing light, air, earth.
Its tendrils endlessly
slap slap slap
blue water into black.

DAWN: CORDOVA BAY, ALASKA

When the shadows (bird-shaped, seal-shaped)
appeared out of that first bruised dawn, we didn't listen
to the cracking from the battles of past winters.

We thought we still lived at the heart of the crystal,
surrounded by ice roses.
Although we smelled the oily hands

abandoning the capsized tanker,
we didn't realise our black pages
would never be white again.

We thought we could open the door
to another north
and the devil would rush by.

But as our cliffs were reduced
to midnight silhouettes,
shotgun smoke coiled above

our slumped bodies in bedrooms
and boathouses; ropes hung
weighted and dripping from rafters.

      In other places,
the land is knocked down by violent winds
or murmurs resignedly

as it swells and blurs with storm.
Places that die every winter are revived
by the returning sun.

But there are no new beginnings
in Cordova Bay:
the last of us

must stand, glistening like chandeliers,
knotted crystal tears on our cheeks,
as the grey snow
falls burning on our hands.

EMBEDDED

I am embedded
in a thousand memos.

A black moon in the sun.
A computer talking to itself.
A division of dreams.
A face of clay. His face. Our face.
A liquidation of light along the Potomac.
A history of madness, a war built on rage.
A whole unknown language. *La ilaha illallah.*
Arrows moving through fog. Authorization. *Nuances.*

Before.
Beating upwards, beyond history, believing everything. *Belonging.*
Beads of water on the windscreen at dawn.
Bent over our desks under small hard suns in the midnight room.
Building invisible cities together.
Bogeymen, queue-jumpers, invaders, as a kind of solution.
Both of us obsessed with being *at the top.*

Collapsing towers.
Comets barked forth by rabid dogs. Spuming smoke.
Confetti blizzards of sorrowing ink. Falling bodies.
Chaos. The world in love with us. Opportunities.
Confrontations sawing beneath the syllables. *Contradictions.*
Crescent moons, children playing with pebbles under olive trees.
Cluster bombs, craters, starfish in the desert.
Co-workers. Collaborators.

Days stepping off into radiant yellow.
Days like silver cylinders.
Dreaming through windows of warrior hills.

Data. Destiny. Deployment. Definite proof
that Saddam Hussein possesses weapons of mass destruction.
Dead spaces growing around the city. Where you can't hear
what anyone is saying.
Duct tape.

Everything hides nothing nicely this year. Even quiet words shudder
in the darkness.
Exasperated trees. A house open to the sky. A tall man
stooping to cradle a broken child.
Ethnic cleansing. Extraordinary rendition.

Falling planes. First flush of passion fading. *Flaws.*

Ghosts locked on my lips.

He watches pornography constantly. He says, It's the perfect moment.
History scuttling out from the white hood, the swastika,
the black dragon scales.
Hearing stories of secret alliances. Holding my feelings tight.
Horrible images of war should not be seen on the front pages.
Human skulls sobbing on the river bank.

If one feels good so does the other, he says.
It hurts, I tell him.

Just words. Just Words. Justwords.

Language as a house of mirrors.
Laws apply only to law-abiding citizens.
Life goes on, he says. There are kiosks at Auschwitz. Dandelions
on the Somme. Movie stars riding motorbikes on the Road of Bones.

Making my way slowly through the office at night.
Mists wreathe the river at dawn. Murmurs trapped in reeds.
Mustard gas.

My language used to be my roof. My walls.
Notebooks of ash.
Nothing between us any more.

Once there was dancing, music.

On his fear of disappointing his father.
On my fear of growing older.
On growing older.
On worries, again and *again*.

Prams in the park.
Photographs of faces pinned to white walls.

Replaced by the not real.
Ragged breaths across the yellow moon.

Shuttered windows.
Scribbles of chalk on the doors of freight cars. Scud missiles.
Stuff happens, he says.

The letterboxes bombed.
The puppet-master never sees the strings in her back.
The toxic fog returning. *There is no bottom to evil.*

The truth in layers, the truth peeled away,
the truth at the empty core.

The wooden people won't go where I tell them any more.

Vanishing pianos.
Vietnam.

We have been deceived getting here. Was it always so?
We decide who comes to this country and the manner of their coming.
Words like maps, like weather.

Wet trees in the park shift and slap against the concrete overpass.
What is this thing called civilization? So ephemeral, so fleeting.
Just an idea, unsteady as a candle flame in dark water.

It doesn't matter if it is true. Soon, it will be.

VOYAGERS

It is impossible to enter this land except under cover
of clouds, through deserts of knives and stakes;
swimming past disappeared bones, bells
with their tongues cut out.

You know that if you close your eyes,
nothing happens. So you lie in the half-eaten shadow
of the concrete wall, try to decipher
the purple and green calligraphy of your new land,

touch the useless fortune folded inside the bracelet
on your arm. Between the shunting trains, smoke
from your cigarette creeps into darkness, climbs
the slipstream.   Lucky voyager.

The black cylinders of storm drains whisper unwelcome
secrets: days lost to bitter-hued bottles, the disappointed
mumble of the freeway,
rats slipping over rusted steel fences,

the brown tongue of water at your feet,
the barbed wire rosettes. I see from your wry grimace
across the tracks, you know you should
have tried this journey when you were 18, when

your life was what you valued least.
Older, it's hard not to jump at the trains' broken
clatter, the funnelled sawings of brakes, the rattle
of the forgotten flagpole above the concrete siding.

You recite poetry to yourself.
The words are fireflies lighting dark gardens.

Trapped in the ribs of night, you remember
threadbare church bells, balsa lanterns trembling
over black corn. The false paper blizzards
that fell from the grey plane nosing the horizon.

Lying for forty days
in seas named only for their colour.

I see you from my carriage as the turning train
flushes the dark from your bedroll.
You smile across half a world,
cheekily raise your hand.

How can I mourn you when I am in such awe
of your tenacious hunger?

~ II ~

A Walk In The World

VACANT LOT

    Dawn light   cloudshadow   gumtree   brown twig
      dew-drop   hoarfrost   ironbark   harpstring

    plumegrass   spiderplant   sandstone   mothvine
      noddingdaisy   mulberry   mealybug   green frog

    log-moss   woodlouse   bull-ant   trapdoor
    lacewing   red worm   fieldmouse   caterpillar

honeybee   blue rim   huntsman   cricket
    slater   fern leaf   purple-top   ladybird

    wagtail   pondweed   fishsack   magpie
      puddle-skater   dragonfly   heartjolt   painted lady

      car tyre   rockpile   hailstones   cobweb
    footprint   raincloud   thorn-nest   owl-light

    firefly   wingbeat   black iris   star-bright
      leaffringe   pearl-drop   moonmask   silence.

IMAGINAL

The pupa hangs
from the slender branch:
a leaf-swaddled doll
who has slept through cycles
of light and dark
until bird call and chance,
heat and slowly
unfurling fern
unleash strange hungers,
vowels of the possible,
in this tilted cradle.

All along, the caterpillar
has housed a trove
of treasure:
the imaginal buds
in this black-nosed papoose
now multiply
with a rush of silver water.

Faint crackling
of the brittle shroud
is the only sound
of escape
as the butterfly pushes
her head and thorax into the dawn.

What is it to have lived a lifetime
and then witness the blue lightning
alchemy of your own birth?

Even the sun,
revolving in its attic of fire,
will never feel this surge
of ecstatic ink.

As the wings harden
in the butterfly's frame,
does she dream
trembling crystal mosaics
in the water-drop she once held
between her limbs?

Does she see a spark rise
in the fleeting day?

NIGHTBIRDS

       July
and the sky is framed and frosted grey.
The temperature has been dropping for days;
the bare wind hums with dead leaves.

Words and concepts peck at my shoulders—
    illumination
        freedom
  persistence
—but they are not birds.

    Above the cold
and unstartable ground:
lightning,
the night garden a chessboard,
a feathered profile spelling *rumination*.

What would it be to transcribe
every thing
without worry, without woe:
a braid of thorns,
the gleam in a maggot's eye?

To be a gatherer of spaces,
a translator of silences,
for whom rumination
never equals defeat.

Beneath the moon
(a bleached heart dangling
from a rusted thread),
the daddy-longlegs

stilts across the shadows.
The powerful owl
turns her disc of rayed feathers.

IN THE LANEWAY

And voices come over the back fences, and the *phttt phttt phttt*
of the sprinkler throwing out streamers of crystals
past the bleached wooden posts
into the shadows
on the cracked path of the laneway.
The shadows are from the trees in the backyards
—there are no trees in the lane—
only tufts of grass between the cracks
and here and there, a yellow daisy
in the windless half-light. If you stretch your neck
you can just see the lucky people in the backyards.
They laugh in the sunlight, the wind lifts their hair,
their clothes are bright squares of colour.
But the ache in your neck means
you cannot strain for long; you drop back
to the hot dirt and look through the shadows
to where the lane rises into a darkness you've never noticed.
You walk past the yards, past entire lives lived
while you were sleeping, toward the slow murmur of the others
at the end of the laneway. But everyone who matters
is further ahead or hasn't arrived. And you wonder,
Was all that writing about the dead a game? As the last crystal drop
disappears without a trace in the dirt at your feet, was it real
or was it a dream?

You wonder, Is the dirt at your feet real? The last crystal drop
disappearing without a trace must be a dream. Maybe
while you were sleeping, everyone who mattered
arrived and went further ahead.
If you walk past the slow murmur from the backyards,
you will surely find the others at the end of the laneway
beyond the rise where the shadows drop into darkness.

You cannot be bothered straining to look into the lives
of the people in their hot backyards: many will be sleeping. Why
stretch your luck when the world here has so many bright squares
of colour: tufts of grass, a yellow daisy. It is odd
the way the dappled shadows shift across the cracks:
there are no trees in the lane.
The windless half-light lies down
on the cracked path. And the stream of pale crystals that wet
the bleached wood posts are unstrung in the laneway. They fall
and are still as the sprinkler goes *phttt ... pht... tt ... ph ...t ... t*
and the voices over the back fences stop.

POLE STAR

In the north,
you dream of home
and the things you've done.
In the north, darkness
bends the straight pale roads,
stars lean away.
In the noon twilight,
sighs of the annual dead
escape through fractures in the snow
and wreathe
your trembling hands.
In the north,
travellers abandon their frozen cars,
burn their broken shoes
for warmth,
denying the flesh-beetles
and worms any shelter.

After years of denying
the flesh-beetle and worm
shelter,
you decide to leave.
After years
of holding others' hands,
telling them that death
will slide over them, warm and inviting,
you kick off your shoes
and wait by the side of the road.

The car that picks you up
takes you further than you want to go.

You spend twilight hours
looking back
as sighs escape
fractures in the snow,
stars lean closer.
I don't know why
I've done
the things I've done
but all roads lead home
in the north.

THE POND-MOONLIGHT

The pond darkens;
the sun is lit knives
between tall straight trees.
The praying mantis hesitates
above the beetle's leaking husk;
the dying bird moves its wing.

The day is a broken wing.
The forest darkens,
the road disassembles, the husk
is pierced by the mantid's knives.
The lost traveller hesitates
beneath the shadowed trees

and stares across the water, foolishly
trying to interpret the unfinished horizon,
the hesitations
between the small breaths in the dark.
As the day bears down on uncompleted lives,
the pines by the pond shudder in the dusk.

The traveller watches night grow from dusk
and sway above the trees.
The mirrored world is scaled with emerging lives:
ants crawl over the bird's splayed wing.
Small breaths from the dark
tremble around the traveller, and she hesitates.

Should she trust her own hesitations?
Around her, ghosts birthed in the dusk
grow with the dark;
they embrace the tall trees,

trail skeletal fingers over dulled feathers, broken quills.
They dissolve into the lives

reflected in the pond. Are these our lives?
Mirrored truths eroded only by our hesitations?
Or are they apparitions trailing broken quills
into the dusk,
pursuing their rival selves between the trees
as the moon darkens?

As the world darkens, the traveller hesitates.
Above the mirrored husks, she moves her shadow wings
and watches the trees become black knives.

TOUCH

Over the past year,
when I visited my mother in the nursing home,
she would hug me as fiercely
as her minnow bones allowed.
    Recently
she has been clinging to me,
a two-handed, white-knuckled grip of my wrist
or arm or waist,
a storm-stricken sailor tethering herself
to a broken mast.

    When she is startled by cupboards,
she takes my hand,
lays it on her cheek,
valiantly resisting
the withdrawing tide
that tugs harder every day.

    As the afternoon is moored,
I one-handedly drink my tea
and eat my plain biscuit.
    And because I feel
cold water around my own ankles,
it is easy to put aside
the misunderstandings
that for decades
made my fingers pull away.
    So I stay,
and we are once again
a little person and a big person
sitting at a low plastic table,
    surrounded by the ghosts

      of teddy bears and dolls
      and a resentful bonneted cat,
staring at the last of the sunlight that falls
through the small window,
      finding fibres of gold in the carpet's wrecked nylon,
      hauling up forgotten relatives and lost homes
and Gran's clever way of cooking quince.
      We hold hands
and listen
to the trees stroking their leaves
in slow whispers against the glass.

LET THE BROKEN

Let every thing
that was ever broken
and every thing that will ever be
stay as they so brokenly are.
Let all the crushed sea-shells remain
in their graveyards of grit,
all the stepped-on flowers, all
the ants and worms and beetles
lie unmourned on their boulevards of dirt.

Do not imagine the dropped cup
stopped in mid-fall, the smashed wine bottle
re-assembling itself, the crumpled car
miraculously expanding.
Do not create elegies for the figure disappeared
from the rear view mirror—to be an adult
is to let forgettings become the links
in our chain of words until
the world is quiescent between breaths.

But on the day
an accidental thrust sends
a little bowl flying,
that lumpy bowl of cracked red mud
with the drooping rim,
that bowl which never sat right,
which perpetually leaned
into its own dusted shadow,
yes on that day
you may get down on your hands
and knees and weep
until red shards flow to the horizon.

DRAGONS

It must be very lonely
to be the last dragon on earth, the only

one foraging for coal on cold mornings.
It must be dispiriting, when your nose is stuffed

with old soot, to call into the distance
and hear nothing but a half-burnt echo rattling

the filleted clouds. How much easier to sit hunched
in your cave, your head under your wing.

To be the one and only sometimes
is not such a good thing.

It is nice to imagine we would spend our last moments
thinking big thoughts. But maybe we would sit all day

gazing into a pond,
stirring the surface with our toenails.

DO NOT READ THIS WALL

The caves etched with charcoal mammoths eating spears are long gone but the prophet with the writing stick still instructs on the wall of your local park: **DO NOT READ THIS.** You read it twice to be sure, before walking on to peruse older bulletins, pastel now in their sandstone rows — *RESPECT* **Che Lives!** *To be thus is nothing*—no-one ever messes with those. Newer scribes unleash red swirls of friendly fire: **eat the rich** *DIG UP YA DOG* erin is confused DARREN IS A SLUT. Disembarked day-trippers refuse to decode these dots and dashes. They retreat to the coach, walking sticks tapping elegies to older signatures: starbursts of wattle in the hatband, bullocks' sad faces lit by lanterns on a pole..... Down the straight path, *love* is nudged by DESTRUCTION; **donald Satan trump** has the reverential space of hard news, while *COPS KILLED JOHNNO !!!* every decade. Beyond rosy joggers and a barking terrier (moulting, like its owner, from an overdose of city), a rebel finger salutes: **O WET CONCRETE, HOW I LOVE THEE.** At the end, a mapmaker blows back incoming dust to chisel a telegram just for you: THIS IS NOT PEACE.

~ III ~

The Animal Kind

EGO AND THE POSSUM

To kneel beside you on the road—
        to be present as darkness coats
        the crooked smoke of passing cars—
is not an act which sanctifies the witness.

To be present as darkness coats the cut gravel
and your tail uncurls, breath by breath,
will not redeem the witness who kneels beside
your spreading red roses.

As I watch your tail become a straightened hook,
a shroud already half unhung,
do the spreading roses reveal
my self in your resin eye?

        Your shroud is more than half unhung.
I think we are both losing the world because
I have always been the black bower in your eye,
the witness who learned nothing.

I cannot make the world come back:
the contract is fixed, the terms clear.
I am the witness who has earned nothing
but the responsibility of laying a hand on every cold flank.

The terms are clear:
what is written on the gravel is not epiphany
but a future of placing a flower in every open mouth—
a radiant bud, a small hope.

There is no epiphany to console the witness;
no apology to justify my presence. The only resurrection
is the small hope which coats the darkness falling in:
that for you the trees will always be coming into bud.

HAWK

Because we are so bound
we long to be taken
to the mountain
to watch you descend
talons gliding
down
down to grasp
that twitching heart on the ground

you rise in a red rush of pulse
and muscle   cold wind   burning beak
you soar   we shed our scars
        enter the singing vast

yet from birth
    time   your only predator
has burdened you
splitting claws
moulting tail-feathers
blurring those twitching hearts
to a tangle
escaping in all directions

          we find you
trapped among the spiny rocks
head turned from
your mate circling above

are you replaying victories
or is it all an echo
      the passions
      the killing

we lever ourselves up
        rise we say
go and winter on the moon
for us

        but we know
soon you'll spread your remnant tail
loosen your claws
retreat under your wing.

RATTLESNAKE

I

In the American southwest
there is a ritual
to the annual killing of rattlesnakes
the ordering of the steel-tipped boots
and wooden barrels
the arrival of the snake handlers
their frenzied calls to the lowering clouds
their spurs branding a dance in the red sand
the staking out of the prairie dog
shaking at the hole
the waiting

      the artful lassoing of the snake
with metal hook and noose
the separation of head and body
elaborate drenching in cold water
the dismembering of every part
into skin   rattle   skull
wallet   key-ring   hucksters' oil

      until the slow sectioning
the drizzling of the grilled flesh
in lemon and butter   the consuming
of death by men with trembling hands

II

The legends are as long as the nine foot
forty pound diamond-head
which gathers its den-mates into a writhing bolus

of three hundred plaited whips
to guard the conquistadors' gold

    it can kill a tree with one strike
    it can live for a year between meals
    a beheaded rattler won't die
    until sundown
    its venom is potent for half a century

the legends lie across the South West
a wedge of storm

III

Must we kill them now
because we did not kill them
in the Garden?
Do we fear them because their poison
makes us forget to breathe?
Because they go willingly into dark places
and yet return
with their faces unchanged?

IV

They go where the heat goes
smelling the air with tongues
    in the desert their black pupils
are slim brackets for their real eyes
    those sensing pits which instantly
gauge the distance between heat and heat
pulse and pulse

    only a cold shovel

        carefully driven by a swaying man
defeats them

V

        Their side-winding S's
are perfect calligraphy across the red desert
when they kill
they are an erotic hallucination
rising
not to inseminate the flailing stars
but to hurl venom at paradise

VI

It is not only humans
who can't resist the urge
to handle fire
        the mare stands
her head swollen to three times
its normal size
blood weeping from her eyes and nostrils
puncture marks on her muzzle

        a triumphant deer will spend an hour
stamping with her hooves
on the rattlesnake's head
        the mockingbird will dive again and again
to tear out those midnight eyes
and the golden eagle
never having heard of Icarus
will fly his prize across the cantaloupe clouds
as his prey dangles, lunges

VII

The rattler's buzz is nothing like a rattle
it is the skitter of bones across concrete
      fingernails flicking at glass
      the contraction of your spine
as you drowse on the warm step.

COYOTE

You slink across desert and snow,
razor-sharp prairie grass,
your lean brown
grey-flecked body merges you
with calderas and stone canyons,
the clefts of mesas.

The craftiness
of your Spanish name
tells you to never covet
the cougar's kill
but you are a master
at driving rabbits
to the edge of territory (you run
at forty miles an hour)
and your murder of rattlesnakes
is an ingenious three-step
pounce and bite and hurl
before joyously falling back
to roll upon the whiplashed scales.

Often
when we return from dropping
our rubbish down the chute,
we take binoculars to the roof
and scan the dusk for your silhouette,
listening through the insects crackling
on the parking lot far below.
As your hilltop lamentations
find your tribes
hidden in the granite,
we raise our own heads
to the emergent moon.

Yet we call you
twilight jackal
when you leave your clefts
and canyons
to nose the city garbage.
      Why do we disparage you,
prairie wolf?
Are we envious of how
you cross vast grey-blue silences,
the dust undisturbed in your wake?
Or are we unnerved
by the suspicion that,
in this second millennium
of our predations,
you are more essential
to the world's balance than we?

PACHYDERM

Walking through the night landscape, carrying
the tonnage of the historical brain, the ivory prize,
griefs of ages. Stepping in time to the night trumpets
of startled birds, savannah grasses sawing beneath
shuddering boabs, the snare-drum growls of the big cats.
Walking colossi with animal faces and plant-like ears,
walking across just-birthed desert places, slow-blinking
against the century's go-go pulse, stroking a wind
mazy with messages, divining a route between razor wire
and smokehouses. Walking down the chain of being
                          into the epoch
of vivisection and dirt pits, walking
grey hides imprinted with zodiacs and song lines,
a millennia of aunties flayed and thrown down
on to polished wood boards. Walking into hollow-hearted
receptacles for umbrellas   walking
carved fancies for wrists and ears   walking   potions and powders
walking back through sacred meat   petty lusts   dinosaur swamps
                      walking while we sleep   walking
mantled by warm dust night   walking   then walking   now walking
never far enough.

~ IV ~

Black Sun

CLIMATE CHANGE

It doesn't look like a sky it looks like milky beer
it doesn't look like a road it looks like a scalded tongue
it doesn't look like mustard gas seeping through
the garden's blackened grass it looks like a zebra in purple light
it doesn't look like a house it looks like a hatchery of bones
something is trying to leave but I cannot see what it is

it doesn't look like a doorway it looks like a gaping mouth
it doesn't look like a living room it looks like a sandpit on fire
it doesn't look like a staircase it looks like a dislocated spine
it doesn't look like a bed it looks like a gutted orchid
something is leaving but I cannot see what it is

it doesn't look like a bloodstain—it's a red bat nailed to the wall
it doesn't look like fingernails on the floor but a scattering
                              of porcelain confetti
it doesn't look like a cat but a shellfish leaping from boiling water
it doesn't look like a young woman searching through bones it looks
            like an old woman searching through sticks of chalk
something has left but I cannot see what it was

it didn't look like a pile of discarded eyes but a bowl of rotting eggs
it didn't look like an amputated finger but a pencil with broken teeth
it didn't look like severed ears but peach halves listening at the door
it didn't look like dissected lips but scarlet butterflies in flight

something has left
and it didn't look human.

HUNTING

Let me tell you about the time
she went running. You were young,
a fraction, still learning how to say nothing.
You probably thought the land was green,
red stars on the bushes, the water turning over
into silver as the swans lifted. You've seen
the photographs. But the earth was already
devouring factories, rusted cars, land mines;
already turning the colour of old lung, sky like marrow.
That was what she ran into.

They said she was disoriented. Disturbed.
*Now that I have everything I need, my life
is unbearable*. She left the group, they said,
muttering about totems, a beast
in all its feathered glory. *I want to hunt
the real*. Only that sounds like her. One must
have a mind for hunting, know the old ways.
They aren't so hard.

She went into the beyond without her identity card.
No longer a citizen. So they said.
She went past the parade of black trees,
the hills like broken kneecaps. The air was full of smoke.
Her equipment hummed uselessly across the dark and bitter plain.

WHAT WE SAY WHEN YOU ASK WHY WE DID WHAT WE DID

Because black fog was frozen
in the tree-tops. Black fog
frozen in apartment blocks.
Endless blue-black nights
heavy with rain.
We told ourselves what was needed
was a new spark: fierce, extreme,
a yellow flame tinged purple, carmine,
green. An agate flame veined indigo
that would blaze up, then
precisely die.

It was not much of a reason, I know. All we can say is
it seemed the right one at the time.

So we brought cauldrons of fire
into our cities. We danced all night, our eyes
clutching at smoke.
When the flames did not precisely die,
we told ourselves only the chosen
should survive the red pour
of knives and silence, incurable
mouthfuls of blood berries,
bandaged eyes.

It's not much of a reason, I know. All we can say is
it seemed the right one at the time.

And now.
       Now there is ash
because every day
we damp the fire down
to skeins of soot and fans of broken white.

Every day we wait for the wind to come
and carry our ash to other cities,
dominions of the unchosen.
It seems like the right decision for the times.

But tonight
the wind carries ash from other fires,
other flames, into the heart
of our domain.
What can we say? It is a blue-black night;
the wind is blowing through tree-tops,
apartment blocks. Blowing
and blowing.

WINDMILL

Strangers who drive through our small town
must think a bomb bit and hissed out
a grey wind, red around the edges. It must have been
more than the sun that bleached
the wooden fences and cattle ribs hugging the fissures,
that devoured the windmill's blades
so it grimaces, gap-toothed,
over the broken-necked tractors.

As the day descends with hammers of heat,
dingoes creep beneath our splintered porches.
The windmill clicks its teeth,
the birds remain on the horizon, the ground
cups our summoned faces.

SOMERSAULTS

We travel toward the horizon, through chasms
                              untouched by starlight.
Behind me, where the forest has become desert
and shopping malls meet canyons,
my sister is doing her somersaults.

Though the forest is desert, my sister will not leave:
she wants to watch the whip grass renew itself,
find someone to somersault with
and welcome every refugee from the sawdust Pacific.

My sister wants to be held as the whip-grass renews itself,
to greet—without a shred of bitterness—
all the dusted and drifting souls
before she is summoned to the horizon.

But I have my duty, shredded by bitterness.
Behind the rusted gate, I call, *Come here,*
let's walk toward the horizon.
And I move wingless in the dark between thoughts.

My sister opens the rusted gate, hesitating
beside the fissured headstones. She peers
at the wingless souls hung in meridian smoke,
searches the dark for storms and white lightning.

Sister! I call. Reluctantly, she glides through
                               the fissured headstones.
I tell her she will have time to see
the storms and white lightning
that once came at noon (and only at noon):

You'll have all of time to look, little sister,

when you come to the last gate.
She joins me at noon (it will always be noon),
and waits to see if orchids blossom in the rain.

I close the gate. We look back as
the derelict malls become desert,
orchids of fire seed the horizon
and falling stars light every chasm.

~ V ~

Poems Written In The Time of Plague

BLUE IN THE TIME OF PLAGUE

I'm thinking of blue
because I just finished reading
about a woman who wrote
fifty poems on *blue* the colour
and the mood although
she doesn't mention
the sound of the *b*
its long slow dolorous echo
or its shape
a foot about to kick something
some one
which is what poetry should do
in the nicest possible way

I shouldn't think that
        poetry must soothe
mind and ear
celebrate the *normal* heart
not incite or rile   not lose friends
by hectoring them about *proximity*
        the choice a loss either way

as Larry Kramer found
crusading against that first great infection
of our youth
or rather
his alter-ego does in the film I'm watching
or more accurately the DVD
        the story is almost over
the rolodex cards
tossed in the drawer
the hectoring friendless sores

have hollowed skin after skin
and I'm back on the dance floor
the plague is in the corner
but we don't know it yet
the carnival beat is shaking the walls
everyone shouts in time
arms flung out
windmills of exuberant hands
because we're all too sexy
for this dance   we'll never smile
this much again
and I'm looking
at Tony's dark eyes
and they are the bluest blue
that ever was.

THE BURN

We can't go forward
can't go back

We drive along the track
the ground burns behind us   scorches hair   skin
eyes

Horses wallabies lyrebirds run beside us
we are in the skeleton land of black bark   bone ash   killer trees
small charred stumps   koalas   bandicoots
                              can't go forward can't go back

The tyres explode   we climb down between smouldering fences
metal-skewered bellies   barbed paws
we yearn for the cool safety of the creek

Blind horses bolt across asbestos fields
they break into embers on the creek bank   become tendrils of smoke
eyeless above the water   they can't look forward can't look back

Furnaces surround us   fire tornadoes
flickering demons whose hearts flank
our only safe place

We stumble and fall toward the glistening black ribbon
where a lone wallaby swims this way and that
swims and swims and sinks

Must go forward   Can't go back

As we lie   shouting   in the hot harrowed water
        the questions we never asked
                turn and turn in a slow whirlpool of wet charcoal.

DAY 5: SECOND CONTACT

It was official policy: the garden was theirs. Belief made the difference. Everyone—every *thing*—inside the walls might think otherwise but it would be self-indulgent to resist. Absolute control was inevitable.

They rolled barbed wire around the garden walls, dispatched the drone with the contract. 'You can trust us,' they shouted through their megaphones, 'the contract of surrender clearly says we will be firm but fair. Besides, a warrior's heart is always bigger.' No sound on the breeze. The drone returned, opened its claws: a small rain of unruly roses and strident grasses. Fragments of paper. They tried again: it was self-indulgent for inside-dwellers to resist—the ones with technology were fittest to rule—scientists had proven their hearts were far bigger.

>Their flags fluttered in the rising wind.
>The drone returned with more, mutinous rain.

Their scientists advocated fire: the nearby river would douse escaping flames. What else could they do? They had to be firm as well as fair: it clearly said so in the contract of surrender. Besides, it made sense to use elementals in such an elemental situation. So they rolled back the wire, sent in the flame-throwers and gasoline: a minor problem smartly solved, with the added fun of seeing it all burn down. Their soldiers went along the blackened paths, past the shrivelled trees. They had a little fun: a few quick rounds of All Fall Down, before raking out the lattice of curled wings on the ground. A lagging conscript was hustled from the corner where those few, puny buds could be ignored—absolute control is inevitable if you have the latest tools.

HOLES

Ever since Davey's death,
rain has pierced
the house with black frozen spears.
Which is why I write to request

your help against the rain impaling
our roof and walls:
I need you to contact
the one who is absent.

It might save the foundations from cracking
if the elders received a message
from the absent one.
A few words would do: *I'm fine, having so much fun!*

Any sentimental message is welcome;
lying is more than acceptable.
Even a single 'fun' might fill the holes
where the foundations used to be.

Here's a message that would relieve: *I'll be home soon
so don't spend your days digging up the garden
for dirt and stones.* All lies are acceptable
when trying to fill the deepest holes:

*Don't spend your nights
searching abandoned lots and train stations for me.
Don't try to fill the hole
that runs to the centre of the world.*

Please advise—the younger ones are exhausted searching

abandoned lots and morgues. My own pages of lies
no longer convince and we have run out of dirt
to fill the hole. The blisters on our hands tell me

pages of words don't fill gaps the way they did.
They can't stop rain piercing the house
or soothe the blisters on our hearts
since Davey died.

HALF THE SKY

You see me sometimes,
a patina
on the clouds, a disbelief.
You cannot imagine
how I stood
for a millennium.

I could tell you
why
I waited so long
in darkness and smoke:
watching
the pageants below
gifted me
the bruises
of a rebel.

But you walk through
my shadow,
oblivious
to the weight
of my task.

Look up:
I only stayed
to claim
my half of sky.
I won't endure
another millennium
of standing silently by.

LISTENING

Run, friend. The grieving grasses are behind you now
and the fallen walls, and the words that told you to weep in silence.

Remember when you sat beside the railway track? You heard
the grasses holding their hurt syllables tight inside
                              the dawn-flushed silence.

The grasses ignored the plague trains that ricocheted
between cities and silence

but they bowed their husky heads to the wind blowing
through the empty factories, over walls ruckled with silence.

Every day, every year, the names painted on the fallen bricks
are strobed by train shadows. Yearning to escape the silence,

they un-suture their grieving syllables and fling them
to Orion, telling us: Run, friend, to the horizon. Flee the silence.

As you run now, do you hear your footsteps strike
a new word – weep – from the silence?

Keep running – can you keep running – and if you can, will you?
Friend, the same dawn fastens everywhere onto the world,
                              the same wind blows silence.

HOLY MOTHER IN THE SUBURBS

      Foetus tails curled beneath

chain-mail clouds.

      Wet-nosed children

stomping on shamrocks,

      young men

close-handed in alleys.

      Every noon,

the obsidian smoke from glass-pipe promises

      brings tears to the painted eyes

of the Mother on the red brick wall.

PEBBLE

To be inside a pebble is to feel
secure but also very cold.
And to realise, as a hand closes
around the pebble, I am alone.

This cold dark offers no security
—you are not with me—
and the hand closed around the pebble
is lifting me, sending me away from you.

Are you not here
because you are in another stone,
travelling toward me?
Will we be struck together, to make fire?

I don't like to think your pebble
could be flung across a barricade, a dusty street,
could be struck against another to burn
the world down.

Your stone should be the one
to bring light.

I wish both of us could be taken
to the same pond on a quiet afternoon
and flung, two pebbles weightless in the world,
skimming across circles of wet sun.

SITTING ALONE

After my daily visit to the nursing home,
I wait on the station platform,
shrouded
in dusk the colour
of bruised plums.

The wind rises,
bending
the first pleats of night.
Strands of spider web—
ghost grey hair—
drift up from the impenetrable trees
beside the railway tracks.

I want to sit forever
cloaked in winter night,
where everything is not as it should be
but is not as catastrophic
as it could be.

I want to sit
counting
my cold breaths
in the moonlight,
heedless as a child again
running through night shadows,
not knowing
what their shapes mean.

I want to have never learned
the lessons of the present.

But the train is here
to take me back
to the city's furnace,
away from these night-lands
where *is*
teeters always
on the precipice
of *isn't*.

And as I do every night,
I fear I will not speak to you again.

MUSIC IN THE TIME OF PLAGUE

Emily Jane Brontë,
    I like to think of you
        walking the moors in late December,
            solo across granite.

You turn from the churched sky,
    the tallow towns, and climb the tors,
        crevice by crevice, cauled
            in crystalline winds.

The moon nods its bruised head,
    beckons you up
        into its adagios of light.
            The hereditary thread tightens.

You let yourself be
    pulled home
        even though you could walk forever
        through the gloaming.

But here,
    it is the end
        of another blazing punitive summer.
            Festering breaths lock us down.

Where are your jewelled peaks, Emily?
    Where are the symphonies
        of wind through wild grasses, the ballads
            of the unfettered creatures?

For us, there is nothing
    but sitting in darkened rooms,
        listening to the radio. Old sweet melodies

     pierce the heart, the lungs.

Emily,
  when I think of you
    walking beyond the desolate songs,
      I turn from my walled horizon,

and follow the music
    of the unfettered creatures, the wild grasses.
     My breaths—my beating heart—are
      bells in the glittering wind.

Where is the beckoning light?

~ VI ~

It Starts Here

Whatever you think you can do or believe you can do, begin it.
Action has magic, beauty and power in it.

—Johann Wolfgang von Goethe

DEMOCRACY

it will not be simple
it will take longer than you thought
it will take all your resolve, all your energy
it will take your heart, your idealism
it will take your friends' loyalties
it will not be quick, it will not be easy

it will be easy, it will be quicker than you thought
it will take a few concessions, a few modifications
it will strengthen your heart, it will increase your energy
it will reduce your cynicism, it will find you new friends
it will be quick, it will be easy

you are planting a flag on the shore of a land not yet explored
you are dreaming every night of arms waving in oceans of hooks
you are alone every night on the road of bones
your dreams are black caskets and no-one can solace you

it will be short it will be simple
it will not be short it will not be simple
it will be temporary
it will not be temporary
this pain
this discovery
this endless
pillaging of graveyards.

NATALYA SAYS THANK YOU

Thank you for this cell
Thank you for this window which frames
    the daily instalment of the most fascinating film
    ever made
Thank you for the stars that hide in plain sight
    glowing   immutable
instructional

Here in Archangelsk
I have peeled off my false self
I no longer titter at the news
the sun is rusting

For years I staggered beneath the weight
of my lip-sticked voice   my diazepam smile
Even when the make-up on my face
turned to scales
I ignored the glass splinters in my throat

I didn't realise
I was already in the gulag
when I found smears of blood on my shoes
after walking through
the mounds of autumn leaves in Crow Park

    So thank you for sending me to the white ward
with the other social parasites
    Thank you for pinning me to the white floor
with the disturbers of peace
    for sending me to this black box
    where time is counted
not by the blows falling on the crowd
    but in the honest drips of water on stone

Thank you for shutting off the power so I can enjoy
      the warmth of the old yellow moon
Thank you for my three unbroken fingers
      the most perfect pens
      for the velvet pages of moss on my walls

      The vultures have been bringing me news
they think will make me pessimistic
Anna A–spiky-handed muse
of every drummer girl–
is playing chess with her shadow
Brodsky has learned to knit with cobwebs
Marina Tsvetayeva is re-arranging
the stains on her ceiling
Nika and Petya, Olga K and Olga P
are extracting warrior songs
from the brown clouds of crying above their drains

We are all eating dirt and it is wonderful
we are drinking mouldy water that tastes like champagne
we are sitting in our unwashed clothes and smelling our own perfume
for the first time
we have resurrected the friend lover daughter son sister brother
mother father
in each of us

So thank you thank you
I will go back to the gulag and stand in Crow Park
to meet myself
I will listen for the falling scales
I will follow the splintered glass.

THREE

Human:
      Don't expect us to be grateful
just because they add a different hue
to the horizon.
      We turn iron inklings
into ships to conquer the stars

but the only thing those earth-imprisoned
collections of leaf and twig know how to do
is stand and brood
and obscure the view.

Even they must admit
they are unwieldy, unpredictable:
      one lives, one dies,
      one is eaten from within.

If they could feel, they would thank us
for creating their legacy—as chairs and flutes,
beams for rooves—when we could easily
whittle them all down, matchsticks
to set their world on fire.

Tree:
      It seems a truth
too obvious to dispute—
we have been here three hundred years,
our ancestors for sixty million more.

Our four thousand year old sister,
hidden in her valley,

still transforms toxic Lilliputian breath
into oxygen.

We shelter the world: see the sugar gliders
in our canopy, the grey and rufous fantails.
Hear the symphony of the chocolate-wattled bat,
the whipbird's call, and pause, and crack.

      Even in our dying days,
our hollow trunks are home to ghost moth
and jewel beetle,
to quietly drumming caterpillar.

The truth is inescapable:
every leaf we shed
reduces the Lilliputians' shade
until the last of them can only stand,

star-conquering iron-shaping
matchstick-wielding owners
of a bare and rocky land.

Revenant from the Future:
      Let me tell you
what I have seen—
a vast lake, an ebonite wind,
an empty shore.

      I have returned
to ask you both:
if some natural order has been broken,
an ancient rhythm contorted,

can we three not invoke that time
when tree-gods gladly

gave up their luscious fruits,
and two-legged beings slumbered
beneath boughs
consecrated with starlight
and sky?

      As we stand on the peak,
the blue grasses undulating around us,
and fling out our arms and feel
the wind stroke our core,
are we so different in our wanting

another day and
another and more?
Can't you see: we three
must take these words from the peak,
lay them down on our graves.

One lives, one dies?
No: one dies,
one dies,
one dies,
one dies,
one dies,
one dies …

THE LAST POEM

The poem could start
with the first garden or first blade of grass—
even the first star flaring beyond a thought
       nature in all its forms
       gods in all their forms
followed by the usual mud and alchemy
flippers turned to hands
fire   sails

Dis-treaties

The sixty-five thousand year old mulch
untouched by hoof
is ploughed away
rocks and clubs become knives and bombs
bricks replace trees
tickets for the beach
sinking rafts and more bombs

       In the crumbling cities
the people kneel before the television
the altar the glittering mall
the tanks
the people wear gas masks in summer
as they search for a blade of new grass
the people are saying
Isn't there a better way?

       The dust is blowing
we're at the epilogue already
We may be too late   It's always too late

Is it too late?
We can go out into the dusty twilight
dream up
our own wild glade

Come among the whispering trees
put your face against the cool bark
write in the black sap
what we hear   what we know

          Dig
into the powdery ground
through all the mute human discards
put a seed in the true earth
plant   grow
It is only too late
for silence.

ACKNOWLEDGEMENTS

Firstly, and above all, a respectful dedication to the Gadigal Peoples on whose lands—which stretch from Sydney's Inner-West to the Harbour—all these poems were written.

The following poems first appeared in these journals:

'Against the Glass': *The Canberra Times* (2019); 'Climate Change': *Meanjin* (2010), *Best Australian Poems* 2010; 'Democracy': *Southerly: Australian Dreams 1* (2014); 'Do Not Read This Wall': *Cordite* (2017); 'Dragons': *The Sun-Herald* (2015); 'Hunting': *Blue Dog* (2008); 'In The Laneway': *Best Australian Poems* 2011; 'Photograph: Sunrise, Syria, August 2017': *2018 ACU Prize for Poetry Anthology: Empathy*; 'Quota': *2014 ACU Literature Prize Anthology: The Language of Compassion*.

'Voyagers' appeared in *Meanjin* (2007) and in the author's second poetry collection *The Searchers* (2014, Island Press). 'Embedded' appeared in the author's debut poetry collection *Ruin* (Interactive Press, 2010).

Longer versions of 'Windmill' and 'Dawn: Cordova Bay, Alaska' appeared in *Mascara Journal* (2009). 'Imaginal' was selected for (the event) The Sawmillers Poetry Prize: Sculpture at Sawmillers Reading Beside the Harbour (2016).

NOTES

The following events inspired the poems listed below:

I. The Hours And The Times

'Photograph: Sunrise, Syria, August 2017.' Written after watching a 2017 Australian television news broadcast which included an image of a young Syrian girl whose dark hair was in pigtails and who was sitting on what appeared to be a hospital cot in a tent. The author has so far been unable to source the image for attribution and dedication. Any information is most welcome.

'Deep Water': The April 2010 explosion of the Deepwater Horizon oil drilling rig in the Gulf of Mexico. Multiple safety systems failed; eleven people were killed.

'Slick': The 2009 Montara oil and gas leak in the Timor Sea, off the West Australian coast. The resulting contamination of Timorese and Australian coasts means the spill is still considered one of the worst in the histories of both nations.

'Dawn: Cordova Bay, Alaska': The 1989 Exxon Valdez Oil Spill, usually rated in the top ten worst spills in history. Billions of birds, fish, seals, whales and other animals were killed or maimed. A 2015 study found evidence of defective growth in spawning salmon.

II. A Walk In The World

'Vacant Lot': Written after reading Robert Francis' list poem 'Silent Poem'.

'Nightbirds': Written after reading Charles Wright's 'Stone Canyon Nocturne', this reworks Wright's line 'The moon, like a dead heart, cold and unstartable, hangs by a thread'.

'The Pond-Moonlight': This non-rhyming sestina was inspired by Edward Steichen's photo-painting of the same name.

III. The Human Kind

'Ego And The Possum' is dedicated to the injured ringtail possum found on Sydney's Bobbin Head Road in September 2018 and to the neighbours, passers-by and the off-duty veterinarian who all came to help, especially the young woman who drove the possum to the Sydney Animal Hospital. A special thank you to all the Hospital's dedicated workers—many of them volunteers.

'Rattlesnake': Written after reading *The Red Hourglass – Lives of The Predators* by Gordon Grice (Delacorte Press: 1998, New York) and multiple American website articles on human interactions with rattlesnakes, dating back to the writing of S. C. Turnbo (1844-1925).

IV. Black Sun

'Climate Change': Styled after Hugh Sykes Davies' 1938 'Poem'.

V. Poems Written In The Time of Plague

'Blue In the Time of Plague' references the title of Right Said Fred's 1992 single *I'm Too Sexy*. The poem also references the title of Larry Kramer's 1985 play *The Normal Heart*.

VI: It Starts Here

The quote 'Whatever you think you can do ... magic, beauty and power in it' has varying translations. At the time of going to print, the quote is attributed to Johann Wolfgang von Goethe.

'Democracy' takes structural inspiration from 'Final Notations' by Adrienne Rich and pivots off that poem's phrases 'it will not be simple ... it will not be long'.

'Natalya Says Thank You'. Lines in this poem engage with the lives and works of several Russian writers:

As noted in the biographical notes in *Against Forgetting: Twentieth Century Poetry of Witness* (ed. Carolyn Forché; W.W.Norton & Company: New York, 1993), Russian poet and translator Natalya Gorbanevskaya was sent to a psychiatric hospital 'of special type' for her civil rights activism.

After being judged a 'social parasite', poet Joseph Brodsky was sentenced to hard labour in the Archangelsk region of Russia. (*ibid.* Forché and archives).

Marina Tsvetayeva's husband was murdered by the secret police and her daughter was twice imprisoned. (*ibid.*)

Veronika 'Nika' Nikulshina, Petya Verzilov, Olga Kuracheva and Olga Pakhtusova are the four members of punk rock activist group Pussy Riot who were re-arrested after protesting at the 2018 World Cup, following imprisonments of other members.

The line 'the brown clouds of crying above their drains' was inspired by the title of Peter Boyle's poetry collection *The Blue Cloud of Crying* (Hale and Iremonger, 1997).

'Three' adapts the three-voice structure of Leigh Hunt's 1836 poem 'The Fish, the Man, and the Spirit'. Stanzas 2 and 3 in "Revenant from the Future" (the final section of 'Three') reference images from the author's poem 'South' (2016).

'The Last Poem' was written at the tail-end of a year (2019) which included:

confirmation in a German study of the catastrophic decrease of insect populations;

reports from America of regional losses of up to 90% of bee colonies in 2017-2018 due to CCD (Colony Collapse Disorder) which occurs when the majority of worker bees disappear from the colony;

floods in the first half of the year in Australia, apocalyptic fires in the second half; budget cuts to NSW National Parks staff; reduced money nationally for (Australian) research, wildlife monitoring and bush-care programmes, and on-going political squabbling, with resulting inertia, over climate change.

In August 2021, the IPCC (Intergovernmental Panel on Climate Change) issued its summary of the impacts of global warming. The report was dubbed 'a code red for humanity' by the United Nations Secretary-General Antonio Guterres.

Cover Image

Cover and title page images are edited versions of "Spoil (Oil Spill)" by S.A. Street Photographer and is licensed with CC BY 2.0. To view a copy of this license, visit https://creativecommons.org/licenses/by/2.0/

Roberta Lowing's poems have been published in *Meanjin, Blue Dog, Overland, Southerly, Five Bells, The Newcastle Poetry Prize Anthology* and *Best Australian Poems*. Her first collection of poetry, *Ruin* (a 55-poem sequence on the Iraq War told in four voices, published by Interactive Press, 2010) was co-winner of the 2011 Asher Literary Award.

Roberta's first novel *Notorious* (Allen & Unwin) was shortlisted for the 2011 Prime Minister's Literary Awards and the 2011 Commonwealth Book Prize. Previously a full-time film critic for Fairfax Media, her other works include *The Sun-Herald and Sunday Age Family DVD Guide* (Fairfax Books).

Roberta published her second poetry collection, *The Searchers,* in 2014 (Island Press). Her 2014 children's book, *My Pet Octopus Is A Top Darts Player*, was published through Wuthering Ink: The Authors Portal.

www.ingramcontent.com/pod-product-compliance
Lightning Source LLC
Chambersburg PA
CBHW022334300426
44109CB00040B/650